Cities

COLORING BOOK

David and La Jeana Bodo

DOVER PUBLICATIONS, INC.
MINEOLA, NEW YORK

Copyright

Copyright © 2016 by Dover Publications, Inc.
All rights reserved.

Bibliographical Note

Cities Coloring Book: Your Passport to Calm is a new work, first published by
Dover Publications, Inc., in 2016.

International Standard Book Number
ISBN-13: 978-0-486-81276-2
ISBN-10: 0-486-81276-6

Manufactured in the United States
81276601   2016
www.doverpublications.com

bliss

\'blis\

noun

1. supreme happiness; utter joy or contentment

2. heaven; paradise

3. your passport to calm

Take a relaxing journey around the world with *BLISS Cities Coloring Book: Your Passport to Calm.* If you're a seasoned traveler or just long to be one, these unique circular ready-to-color designs of the planet's greatest cities will truly expand your horizons. And you can now travel to your newly found retreat of peace and serenity whenever you'd like with this petite-sized collection of sophisticated artwork.

Amsterdam

Bangkok

Barcelona

Berlin

Boston

Buenos Aires

Cairo

Capetown

Cartegena

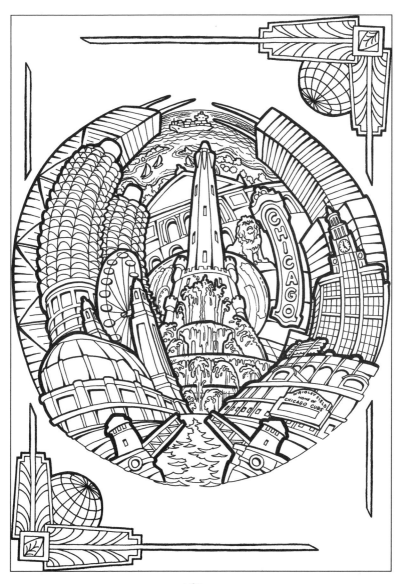

Chicago

Denver

Dubai

Dublin

Edinburgh

Golden Triangle

Havana

Hong Kong

Honolulu

Istanbul

Jerusalem

Las Vegas

Lisbon

London

Los Angeles

Madrid

Mexico City

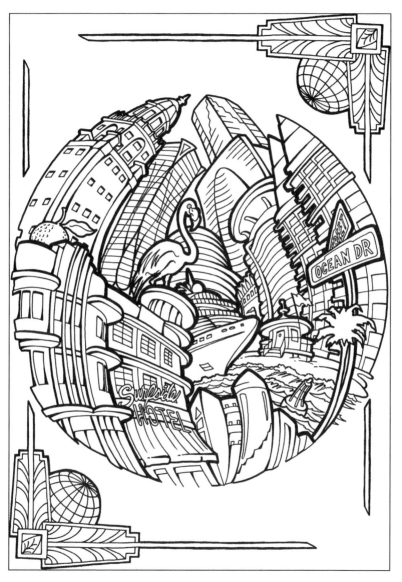

Miami

Montreal

Moscow

New Orleans

New York

Paris

Prague

Rio de Janeiro

Rome

Saint Petersburg

San Francisco

Seoul

Shanghai

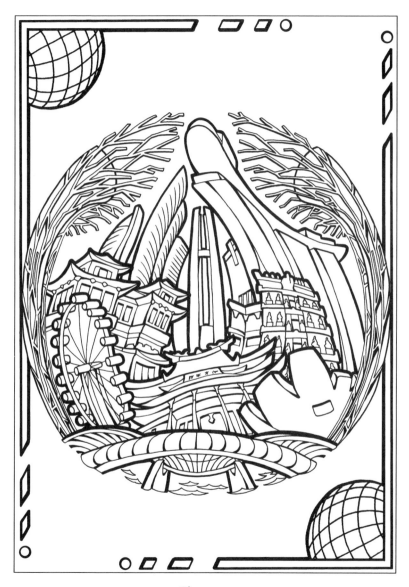

Singapore

Sydney

Tokyo

Vancouver

Venice

Vienna

World